Orcas of the Salish Sea

Alaska

British
Columbia

CANADA

UNITED STATES

Washington

Oregon

California

Pacific Ocean

Home waters

Range

MARK LEIREN-YOUNG

Orcas of the Salish Sea

ORCA BOOK PUBLISHERS

Onyx breaching near the Fraser River, where the chinook swim. GARY SUTTON

ONYX is one of the world's most famous whales. He lives in the Salish Sea in the Pacific Ocean.

Onyx is part of a community called southern resident orcas. They spend most of their time off the coast of Washington and British Columbia. Southern residents are superstars. They have been watched, studied, photographed and filmed more than any other wild whales in the world!

SOUTHERN RESIDENTS swim back and forth between the United States and Canada. Whales don't know our borders. Whale communities are called pods because whales stick close together, like peas in pods. When two or more southern resident pods meet, they line up to say hello. After they greet each other, the pods swim together. We call that a superpod! It's an orca party.

Hy'Shqa spy-hopping in front of orcas from J pod and L pod in the Strait of Juan De Fuca. BRENDON BISSONNETTE (EAGLE WING TOURS)

Bigg's matriarch T37A hunting a harbor porpoise near the north end of Orcas Island. CLINT RIVERS

WHEN SCIENTISTS STARTED STUDYING these orcas in the wild, they gave each pod a letter so they could tell them apart. There are three southern resident pods: J, K and L. Scientists also gave each whale a number. Over the years more than 40 orcas have been counted in K pod, more than 50 in J pod and over 120 in L pod. But in 2019 there were fewer than 75 southern resident orcas.

The pod we know best is J pod. J pod whales always make waves!

Southern resident orcas stay with their pods for their entire lives. The resident boys always swim at their mom's side. Their mothers help them survive. Male residents don't live long without Mom to look after them. Onyx was born in 1992. After his mother, Olympia, died, Onyx surprised human scientists by leaving L pod and joining K pod!

ONYX ADOPTED two new mothers—Lummi and Georgia. After they died, Onyx surprised the experts again when he left K pod and joined J pod! That's where Onyx met Granny, the oldest whale in the Salish Sea. Scientists named her Granny because they knew she was a grandmother. In orca society mothers lead the families. The eldest female leads the pod.

Communities led by females are called matriarchies. When Onyx started swimming with her, Granny was the matriarch of J pod and all the southern residents. Granny starred in books and movies. She was loved by many people in Washington State. She was elected honorary mayor of Orcas Island. There's a street named after her on San Juan Island. Some people think she was over 100 years old when she died. After Granny died, Onyx stayed with J pod.

Onyx and Granny hanging out together in the Salish Sea. VAL SHORE

Granny breaching at sunset off Race Rocks in BC. CLINT RIVERS

Bigg's orcas off the coast of Vancouver Island. SERGIOBOCCARDO/ISTOCK

ORCAS COMMUNICATE using sounds we call vocalizations. We don't know if orcas have words like we do, but we know they understand each other. Each pod has its own unique vocalizations. Orcas also have a superpower called echolocation. They send out sound waves that bounce off everything nearby. These waves show orcas the world around them. Echolocation is whale sonar.

Onyx spy-hopping in Active Pass. GARY SUTTON

SOMETIMES ORCAS LIKE ONYX see the world by poking their heads above the waves to watch what's going on. It looks like they are balancing on their tails. We call this spy-hopping. We don't know what they call it!

A J pod orca checking out the view off the coast of Everett, Washington. JANINE HARLES

ORCAS ALSO WATCH THEIR WORLD by jumping so high out of the water that it's like they're flying. This is called breaching.

Onyx exploring the Salish Sea. GARY SUTTON

BECAUSE SOME TYPES OF ORCAS hunt other whales for food, orcas like Onyx used to be called killer whales. Even though we call them killers, they never eat us. Today most people call these whales orcas because it sounds friendlier. This is kind of funny because the word orca comes from the Latin name *Orcinus orca*, which means "demon from hell." Does Onyx look scary to you?

THERE ARE ORCAS IN EVERY OCEAN.

Orcas around the world are different shapes and sizes, depending on where they live and what they eat. Orcas in Norway are hungry for herring. Sometimes they catch herring by following fishing boats and their nets. Sometimes they catch herring by blowing bubbles to make their own nets.

A Norwegian orca on the move! ALESSANDRO DE MADDALENA

A Norwegian orca hunts herring near a fishing boat. ALESSANDRO DE MADDALENA

A superpod of Gerlache (Type B) orcas in the Gerlache Strait. ROBERT MCGILLIVRAY/GETTY IMAGES

SOME ORCAS IN ANTARCTICA HUNT PENGUINS. These orcas are smaller than most others, and their skin is yellow because of algae. These whales are called Gerlache orcas because they are found in the Gerlache Strait. If you're a penguin in the Antarctic, Gerlache orcas *are* killer whales!

A great white shark breaching on a seal-shaped decoy in False Bay, South Africa. ALESSANDRO DE MADDALENA/SHUTTERSTOCK.COM

ORCAS ARE THE MOST POWERFUL PREDATOR in the water. Some African orcas eat great white sharks. Many people think great white sharks are the most dangerous animal in the ocean. Orcas aren't impressed. They catch these sharks by flipping them over so they can't swim.

Orca breaching while hunting a dolphin in False Bay, South Africa. CHRIS & MONIQUE FALLOWS/NATURE PICTURE LIBRARY/ALAMY.COM

SOUTHERN RESIDENTS LIKE ONYX love chinook salmon. All orcas are fussy about what they eat. If their mothers didn't teach them to eat something, it's not on their menu! There are other types of orcas in the Salish Sea besides southern residents. Bigg's orcas eat mammals. Offshore orcas prefer to dine on sleeper sharks.

Chinook salmon spawning in a river near the Salish Sea. RANDIMAL/GETTY IMAGES

Orcas on the hunt for Chinook salmon in the Salish Sea. CLINT RIVERS

THERE IS ONLY ONE SPECIES that harms orcas—humans. Sometimes we hurt them by accident, through polluting their homes. Sometimes we take all their food. Some people have hunted orcas to eat them. Some people have hunted orcas to put them on display.

A male Bigg's orca makes a heart with his blowhole near Sidney Island. CLINT RIVERS

IN 1964 A FOUR-YEAR-OLD ORCA was caught by accident near Vancouver, British Columbia. The local aquarium named him Moby Doll. He was the first orca in captivity. Scientists came from around the world to study Moby. Many years later researchers learned he was a member of J pod. How did they find out? They listened to old recordings, and Moby sounded like the rest of J pod!

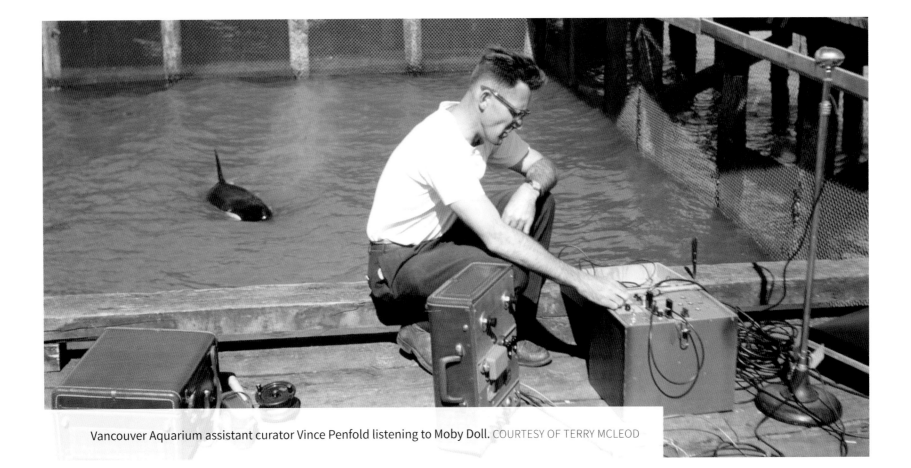

Vancouver Aquarium assistant curator Vince Penfold listening to Moby Doll. COURTESY OF TERRY MCLEOD

Scarlet flying through the air on the night she was learning to breach. CLINT RIVERS

MOBY MADE THE SAME SOUNDS as Scarlet, a J pod whale who Onyx swam with. Scarlet got her name because her mother, Slick, had trouble giving birth to her, and other orcas used their teeth to help, leaving Scarlet with scars. Granny was probably one of the helpers. Maybe Onyx helped too. Scarlet loved to leap out of the water. She was famous for her breaches. Even small orcas can make a huge splash!

When Scarlet was almost four, she got sick. Scarlet and her family weren't getting enough salmon. Veterinarians and scientists tried to help. They couldn't save her. Scarlet's story inspired people to do more to protect orcas in the Salish Sea.

A trio of southern resident orcas in the Johnstone Strait off the coast of Vancouver Island. JURITT/SHUTTERSTOCK.COM

SOUTHERN RESIDENTS LIKE ONYX need more salmon. Orcas everywhere need cleaner, quieter oceans so they can keep swimming and spy-hopping and flying. Many people are trying to make the oceans better for orcas. You can help too. If enough people help, there will always be orcas.

Author Note

As I write this, Onyx is still swimming with J pod. The Canadian and American governments are doing more to help save the endangered southern resident orcas. But the orcas are still starving, still getting sick and facing new threats like increased tanker traffic. These orcas need more chinook—a salmon that is becoming scarce because of overfishing and pollution. Orcas everywhere need food, clean water and quieter oceans. Boaters need to slow down and keep their distance so the orcas can hear what's happening underwater and find their food. Governments work for you. Let them know you care about the future of these wonderful wild orcas. For more on the southern residents and orcas around the world, visit orcaseverywhere.com.

FOR J POD—THE AWESOME ORCAS WHO ALWAYS MAKE WAVES. —M.L.Y.

Cataloguing in Publication information available from Library and Archives Canada

Issued in print and electronic formats.
ISBN 9781459825055 (hardcover) | ISBN 9781459825062 (PDF) | ISBN 9781459825079 (EPUB)

Library of Congress Control Number: 2019947377
Simultaneously published in Canada and the United States in 2020

Summary: Illustrated with stunning photographs, this nonfiction picture book introduces readers to Onyx. He's a member of J pod, the famous family of southern resident orcas off the coast of British Columbia and Washington.

Orca Book Publishers is committed to reducing the consumption of nonrenewable resources in the making of our books. We make every effort to use materials that support a sustainable future.

Orca Book Publishers gratefully acknowledges the support for its publishing programs provided by the following agencies: the Government of Canada, the Canada Council for the Arts and the Province of British Columbia through the BC Arts Council and the Book Publishing Tax Credit.

Cover photos: Jeroen Mikkers/Getty Images
Endpaper map by David Leversee
Design by Rachel Page

ORCA BOOK PUBLISHERS
orcabook.com

Printed and bound in South Korea.

23 22 21 20 • 4 3 2 1

Scarlet swimming with her mom, Slick, in the waters near Washington. KATY LAVECK FOSTER/NOAA FISHERIES PERMIT #18786

The waterways in the Pacific Ocean along the coast of southern British Columbia and northern Washington State are called the **Salish Sea**. In 2009 officials in the United States and Canada chose the name to honor and acknowledge the Coast Salish people of British Columbia and Washington.